HISTORY OF MODERN AFRICA

A BRIEF OVERVIEW FROM BEGINNING TO END

HISTORY ENCOUNTERS

photo on right: Chris Hartford from London, UK, CC BY 2.0 Wikimedia Commons

History of

Modern Africa

A Brief History from Beginning to the End

History Encounters

CONTENTS

Bonus Downloads

Want to Fill Your Digital Library for Free?

Every purchase comes with FREE bonus downloads!
Download yours now by clicking the 'Get it Now' button.

Get it Now

Scan Your Phone to open QR code

Chapter One
Introduction

It is said that all life originated in Africa. This is believable because the continent is rich with minerals and weather that is easy for humans to adapt to. Modern Africa is currently split into different regions: North, West, East, Central, and Southern Africa (not to be mistaken for South Africa). Each region has its own unique stories and extremely rich history. In fact, one of the few things that are common among all African countries is the tradition of storytelling. The stories vary from nation to nation, from tribe to tribe, and from tradition to tradition.

Modern Africa is an amalgamation of many stories that make a coherent tale. Still in the process of evolving and developing, Africa is full of young nations as well as ancient civilizations.

From countries with stories old enough to be mentioned in the Bible to the youngest nation formed in 2011, it contradicts the belief that Africa is the same from one end of the continent to the other. Despite its many struggles, civil wars, and fights for freedom: Africa always moves in a direction that people cannot predict. Zimbabwe, a country notorious for hyperinflation and poverty, now has villagers who use smartphones because of the aspirations of an African tech millionaire called Strive Masiyiwa, while Nigeria has citizens making their first (fully functional) vehicles out of scraps from junkyards, Kenya has growing entertainment industry endearingly called Malaicha Entertainment.

Modern Africa is a testament to the fact that circumstances and society should not be the measures that determine how people are viewed. Much of the continent is still suffering from the repercussions of having been under colonial rule and the continued interest from countries around the world to control its mineral wealth. Some speculate that originally Africa should have gone in the way of modern America, Australia, and Canada in the sense that the indigenous people would become a minority and people would identify Africa as a "white country." But that ended up not happening, and the indigenous people of

Africa had to learn to integrate with various people, some being descendants of colonizers and people that had been ferried from their original countries by colonizers.

Integration and progress can take a hot minute to become fully functional after a hostile beginning, but Africa is making strides toward better human rights and economies. In fact, South Africa, despite having suffered from apartheid, is currently known as a rainbow nation, with people from all over the world finding that it is quite diverse, and despite allegations of xenophobia, most South Africans are very friendly and accommodating.

But one cannot also turn a blind eye to the corrupt governments that keep the people oppressed in many countries, rigged elections, and civil wars that still currently savage the continent. At the same time, even the United States went through stages of civil war, poverty, and unrest before it established itself as a world power. The idea of any country in Africa being a world power eventually is laudable to some people, but one never knows what the future may hold.

Chapter Two

North Africa

North Africa is located in a thin strip of land nestled between the hot deserts of the Sahara and the blue seas of the Mediterranean. It covers the Moroccan Atlantic up until Egypt. There are no real borders about where it starts and ends, making its borders speculative. The earliest known humans lived in North Africa in 260,000 BC. North Africa is known to have one of the largest Arab and Muslim populations in Africa. Historically speaking, the Middle Eastern Arabs invaded the Maghrib (land of the setting Sun), establishing Islam within the 7th to 11th centuries. This has made North Africa a predominantly Muslim region up until modern times, although there are also strong groups of Christians and Jews as well(the Jewish population is largely concentrated in Ethiopia.) Even though there were largely Arabic influences, it also went under the imperial and colonial control of France, the United Kingdom, Spain, and Italy, leaving it under some form of European control until the region gained its independence from the 1950s to the 1960s. Ethiopia is known to be the only African country that was never truly colonized during that time.

North Africa has been mentioned since time immemorial, including in the Bible. Multiple societies' influences have resulted in a rich modern culture. There is a common sentiment that Christianity was brought to Africa by European colonizers, but the existence of the Ethiopian Orthodox Tewahedo Church proves otherwise. The Bible mentions North Africa multiple times, showing that it was a religious center for many millennia. Because of its significance in many religions, North Africa is a center for religious tourism. Because many of the nations in North Africa are Muslim, it is also a safe space for many Muslims to travel to.

North Africa was one of the first regions in Africa to gain freedom from colonialism and had more freedom and benefits than their counterparts did. This might be because by the time the southern and central parts of Africa began to fight for freedom, the colonizers were weary and willing to fight back with more violence and resources. That can be evidenced by the system of apartheid that South Africa would have to overcome versus what other countries went through.

North Africa was traditionally largely involved in trade with ancient civilizations, a legacy carried on to the modern day, with one-third of Africa's GDP being generated in North Africa. Many countries in North Africa tend to identify more with the Middle East than the rest of the continent.

Chapter Three

West Africa

West Africa consists of sixteen countries: "Benin, Burkina Faso, Cape Verde, The Gambia, Ghana, Guinea, Guinea-Bissau, Ivory Coast, Liberia, Mali, Mauritania, Niger, Nigeria, Senegal, Sierra Leone, Togo, as well as Saint Helena, Ascension, and Tristan da Cunha." West Africa was a large economic area throughout history, with different areas being prominent in trade with the Dhar Tichitt, then Djenne-Djenno, the Ghanaian empire, the Mali Empire, etc. West Africa's countries were largely colonized by the British, French, and Middle East. West Africa was where the Atlantic slave trade was concentrated, where thousands of Africans were traded away as cheap colonial labor to European and American slave traders. Some of the empires would purposefully wage war against each other to supply slaves as demand grew immensely, and they found it an easy way to amass a great amount of wealth. Eventually, American, European, and Haitian governments passed laws effectively ending the Atlantic Slave Trade. The slave trade and subsequent scramble for Africa would have long-lasting effects on the stability of West Africa.

The first country to gain independence from colonization would be Ghana. It would be the leader in other African countries actively getting independence creating a domino effect that would move from West Africa to North and East Africa to Central Africa, eventually ending at the tip of Africa in South Africa. The most well-known country in West Africa is Nigeria. Today, Nigeria is constantly on the brink of civil war. Nigeria has established itself as one of the major financial hubs of Africa, contributing greatly to its GDP. The Nigerian entertainment industry is world-renowned, and with the advent of TikTok and Netflix, people are more interested in African cultures and food than ever. Their introduction is often to Nigerian culture. Nigerian cuisine, such as egusi soup, garri, and jollof rice.

West Africa has also become a hub for online scams, with people reporting that many love scammers use public wifi and internet places to complete love scams and other scams. When a documentary was made about what motivates the love scammers in Nigeria and Ghana to do what they do, they stated that generations ago, the "white people" took their people and land, so they were justified in committing crimes against westerners. This was met with widespread disgust from many people around the world. It has been proven that many of the funds sent to live scammers are also used to fund mafia and terrorist syndicates in West Africa. West Africa is a confusing mixture of insane amounts of wealth (with Nigerians having a sizable amount of the billionaires in Africa) amidst gross amounts of poverty. In places such as the Gambia, poverty causes women to delve into sex work, creating a problematic form of tourism for the region…sex tourism. The Gambia is known to be the hottest sex tourist spot in Africa at the moment. Oftentimes it is the poorest who use whatever resources they have to leave their country in hopes of a better future abroad while the rich live in disproportionate wealth.

Chapter Four

East Africa

East Africa consists of the present countries of Tanzania, Kenya, Uganda, Rwanda, Burundi, the Democratic Republic of Congo, and South Sudan. Djibouti, Eritrea, Ethiopia, and Somalia can also be considered parts of East Africa but are more commonly referred to as the "Horn of Africa." Archeologists believe that the first anatomically modern human beings originated from East Africa. One of the earliest people to be recorded to have lived there were the Khoi-San tribes until the Bantu expanded into East Africa and made contact with the Austronesian and Arabic-speaking settlers. The Arabic settlers spread Islam to the Bantu tribes, but most of the Bantu stuck to their traditional African religions.

The first Europeans to explore East Africa were said to be the Portuguese, who explored what is Kenya and Tanzania today with Vasco de Gama. Portugal wanted to take control of the spice trade from the Arab traders who dominated the area. East Africa became a hotspot for the Scramble for Africa as its ports were useful for trade, and every European country wanted to gain control of them.

East Africa in the modern day is still a major trade route. Many ports are situated there where people from all over Africa go to collect their goods. Tanzania has been a strong port for the transport of Japanese vehicles to various parts of Africa.

Chapter Five

Central Africa

Central Africa consists of the "Central African Republic, Angola, Cameroon, Chad, Equatorial Guinea, Gabon, São Tomé and Príncipe, and Burundi. Cameroon, the Central African Republic, Chad, the Republic of the Congo, Equatorial Guinea, and Gabon) are members of the Economic and Monetary Community of Central Africa," abbreviated as CEMAC. They use a common currency called the Central African Franc, similar to the system established in the European Union with the Euro.

The Sao civilization flourished from the 6th century until the 16th century living by the Chari river. Central Africa would have many empires that dominated during different times, such as the Kanem Empire, Bornu Empire, Shilluk Empire, Baguirmi Empire, Wadai Empire, Lunda Empire, and Kongo Kingdom. During the scramble for Africa, the French and the British would argue over territory until there was an agreement to separate the regions into British West Africa and French West Africa. French West Africa would be what we currently know as Central Africa.

Central Africa is a hub of many activities, and being along the equator also contains some of the greatest riches of Africa, particularly the Democratic Republic of Congo. Unfortunately, Central Africa is often also the home of Ebola. There are many tribes in Central Africa

Chapter Six

Southern Africa

Southern Africa should never be mistaken for South Africa(the country), although South Africa is one of the countries that make up the region. Other countries that are part of Southern Africa are Zimbabwe, Zambia, Namibia, Malawi, Mozambique, Angola, Eswatini, Lesotho, Botswana, Madagascar, and Mauritius. Madagascar is often not included in the mix because its systems and history are distinctly different from the rest of the Southern African region. This is largely due to it being an island nation. Together they formed the Southern African Development Community, which also includes Seychelles.

Many prominent kingdoms would rule, including the kingdom of Mapungubwe, the Kingdom of Zimbabwe, the Torwa Kingdom, the Xhosa Empire, the Ndwandwe Kingdom, the Zulu Kingdom, The Merina Kingdom, and the Mthethwa Paramountcy. During the colonial era, the countries were predominantly controlled by the British, but certain countries were colonized by the Portuguese such as Angola and Mozambique, while Namibia was a German colony. The last country to gain freedom from colonialism was South Africa in 1994.

During its time, the Kingdom of Zimbabwe was known as a major trading center dating back to the Phoenician era. Much of the history of the Kingdom of Zimbabwe was lost during the reign of South Rhodesia. Rulers like Ian Smith promoted the idea that black people could not self-govern and were not capable of a society that was as complex as Great Zimbabwe. Those same sentiments were shared by the apartheid regime in South Africa. It's not surprising to find out that South Rhodesia was a major supporter of apartheid in South Africa. When England imposed sanctions on Southern Rhodesia, South Africa continued to support the Rhodesian government, and the apartheid regime's time grew shorter. Then independence was gained, and South Rhodesia became Zimbabwe.

Countries that were colonized by the British in Southern Africa did not experience much turmoil after colonization in the sense that they have not had any major civil wars won't the worst being xenophobia in South Africa. Countries such as Malawi and Mozambique. Mozambique, in particular, has been under the siege of rebels and Muslim extremists. Botswana is possibly the most successful of all the southern African countries, with a generally peaceful, stable government and currency. They are the only population in the world with a higher number of cows than people. Their currency is the strongest in Southern Africa.

Modern Southern Africa has also distinguished itself in international sports and competition, with the South African rugby team, the Springboks, ranking in the top five teams in the world. Zimbabwe has had citizens compete and win the Olympics. South Africa has had a bevy of women compete in international modeling pageants, with the most recent win being ZozibiniTunzi, who was crowned Miss Universe 2019.

Bonus Download

Want to Fill Your Digital Library for Free?

Every purchase comes with FREE bonus downloads!
Download yours now by clicking the 'Get it Now' button.

Scan Your Phone to open QR code

Chapter Seven

The Scramble for Africa

Cecil John Rhodes is considered a great historical figure by Westerners and one of the vilest men to have ever graced the planet by Africans. He was the first to see the wealth that Africa held and wanted to harness it for his business by using unscrupulous methods to make the non-English speaking, reading, and writing tribes of Africa sign off their rights to land and freedom using underhanded methods. The borders of modern African countries were determined by which European country would take over which part of Africa. Their strategy was to put warring tribes in similar territories so they would be too distracted fighting each other to pay attention to the Europeans. During their planning, they thought of the African tribes as simple-minded people who would never be able to organize themselves into groups that could join together and actively resist them. The territories would be divided among Austria-Hungary, Belgium, Denmark, France, Germany, Great Britain, Italy, the Netherlands, Portugal, Russia, Spain, Sweden-Norway, Turkey, and the United States of America. Many of these countries would lose their territories after World War II as reparations. The rest would have to let go after the UN charter that countries should have a right to choose who governs them.

Chapter Eight

The Beginning of Decolonization of Africa

Before World War II, it was evident that the locals in Africa were very dissatisfied with the state of affairs in their countries. Workers' unions were forming, and African voices were being given a platform on media where they canvassed for their independence, proving that the stereotypes that colonists used to keep them oppressed were largely unfounded and biased. Islam and Christianity, the dominant religions at the time, opposed the systems of a racially divided nation. These attempts to break down colonialism in various countries weren't fully organized or impactful before the 1930s. At this point, no European power was thinking of evacuating their African territories.

Many Africans were conscripted during World War II, which gave Africans more political awareness and the realization that freedom would not come peacefully more likely. It also taught that "the white man" was as vulnerable as any other person and that when in times of trouble, the colonizers were able to treat them as equals if they had to. During the war, they had been comrades, but as soon as the war ended, they were considered lesser humans again. They were not given benefits and rewards for their part in the war like their white compatriots.

After World War II, America would put pressure on England to follow the stipulations of the Atlantic Charter. The Atlantic Charter states that the people of a nation should have the right to choose the government that rules over them. Although Britain was forced to agree to the Charter, Winston Churchill rejected the idea of self-determination for subject nations. Churchill knew that Britain surviving the war had largely been to resources that it had siphoned from its territories.

Despite Britain being reluctant to give self-determination and governance to their territories, India's nationalist movements started all over the nation, giving inspiration to the African nations. During World War II, a non-white country, Japan humbled the European powers by almost effortlessly taking over British domains such as Singapore. Part of colonialism had been the idea that people of European descent were innately better than any other group of people in the world. There have been many renditions by Africans who survived the colonial era that they were taught that white men had all-seeing eyes and were all-powerful. This was reinforced by a disparity in education systems where Africans were simply taught trades such as gardening and sewing while people of European descent were taught more academic pursuits or, at the very least, learned to read and write. The Second World War ended up revealing the weaknesses that colonialism had tried to conceal.

The emergence of the United States as a superpower was also a catalyst at the start of decolonization. From the American standpoint, European imperialism was the leading cause of two world wars up until that point. European countries that had been in top form before the war were now in a vulnerable position, while the United States' location had protected it from taking the bulk of the damage. This gave the States power over the European nations. Inevitably the end of the Second World War would be the beginning of freedom for Africa.

Chapter Nine

The Fight for Freedom

Many European countries were exhausted postwar. At this point, they began to rely more heavily on their colonies and treated them more as places where they wanted to settle down permanently. They noted that the quality of life significantly improved in some colonies, as was the case of the Europeans who settled in Southern Rhodesia (modern-day Zimbabwe). They were known to have vast fields and farms that the English would be shocked by when they found out the extent of their wealth, and that would contribute heavily to the English public approval to sanction systems in Africa that disallowed locals to have self-governance.

England had substantially more resources than other colonial countries, so the countries with British settlers tended to develop better. France had wanted to do the same but was left economically wrecked after the war, as well as Portugal. Initially, the plans of decolonization were meant to have joint governments where Europeans and Africans would rule together. This, in theory, seemed like a peaceful way to resolve the situation, but the Africans would not have it, as would be evidenced in South Rhodesia, Algeria, and Kenya. African nationalists would not have it. Their vision was to have full control of their countries back and for anyone who was not of African descent to live under their governance and not vice-versa. Their reasoning was that they had not asked for the colonists to come and occupy their land, and they had proved capable of being unfair in governmental decisions towards indigenous Africans, so they should be stripped of all power.

Italy would be one of the first European powers to lose all its colonial territories even though it desperately lobbied to keep them. But their territories were lost as part of its punishment for its involvement with Germany during World War II. This would include Libya. Somaliland, Eritrea, and, although never fully their territory, Ethiopia.

Ghana became the very first African colony to gain independence on March 6, 1957, led by Kwame Nkrumah, who stated that "we believe in the rights of all peoples to govern themselves. We affirm the right of all colonial peoples to control their own destinies. All colonies must be free from foreign imperialist control, whether political or economic." The British initially did not want to concede, leading to conflicts in the 1940s and the imprisonment of Nkrumah until Britain, amidst rising nationalism, conceded peacefully for Ghana to have self-governance.

Under Prime Minister Harold Macmillan, who would give a speech on "the Winds of Change" in Africa, people would put into perspective what was happening in Africa. France was fighting a prolonged war in Algeria, and the British could see that it no longer had the resources to do that. Under his guidance, decolonization began to advance rapidly. Britain granted all of its colonies freedom in 1968 except for Southern Rhodesia. Many settled communities would try to fight against Britain's "betrayal." This would lead Britain to impose sanctions on those that refuse to give the locals governance. The regime in Southern Rhodesia and South Africa would be the last to fall.

Chapter Ten

African Countries After Independence

The ramifications of the regimes that countries suffered under colonialism would leave a lasting effect on African countries. The biggest problem with Africa was the issue that its borders had been determined by Europe. The strategy that had been used was to put warring tribes on the same borders so that they would be too busy fighting each other to pay attention to them. They didn't anticipate that the warring tribes would eventually come together to overthrow them. When the countries then attained independence, they were faced with the issue of tribalism.

African identity is not from one's country much as it is from one's tribe. Many civil wars would emerge and still continue to emerge due to problematic borders. One such war would be the Nigerian-Biafran War of 1967-1970, where the Igbo people of Biafra tried to break away from the rest of Nigeria and establish their own state. It's known that the Igbo people are at odds with the largely Muslim Hausa-Fulani people and weren't on the best terms with the Yoruba either. The country of Biafra would never be acknowledged internationally, and the Biafrans would lose the war. This did not solve the issues that they had. Until today, Igbo people identify as Biafrans, and there is always a threat that another civil war might happen for Biafra to break free.

A similar situation looms in Zimbabwe, where the tribes of the Shona and Ndebele were put together in one country. Historically speaking, these countries had been at odds with one another for decades. Soon after Zimbabwe gained independence, the Shona tribe members ousted much of the Ndebele people and parliament members, creating governmental dominance for the Shona. Under the guise of eradicating terrorist groups that still wandered, Robert Mugabe (who identified as Shona) led an attack against the Ju Ndebele known as Gukurahundi, which was basically the mass slaughter of Ndebele people in the

Matebele region of Zimbabwe. Since then, the Ndebele of Zimbabwe has wanted to separate from the rest of the country like Biafra tried but lacked the resources or numbers to execute that. Until today there are still tensions between the Shona and Ndebele tribes of Zimbabwe.

One of the most brutal and shocking conflicts would be the Rwandan genocide. The history of the Hutu and Tutsi is complex, but basically, throughout the beginning of the reign of the Kingdom of Rwanda, the Hutus had dominance. Even as they moved from one colonial power to another, the Hutus would establish a relationship with those in power to retain power. This led to the other tribes of Tutsi and Twa being disenfranchised. The Hutu also made up about 85% of the population of Rwanda. The Belgians supported the Hutus killing off the Tutsis during their period, which led to many Tutsis fleeing the country. The Tutsis would always want to return to their motherland though, which would eventually lead to Tutsis who had fought in the Ugandan war to invade Rwanda. The backlash would be so violent that it would shock the world, and millions of Tutsis would be massacred without mercy using guns, machetes, and anything that could maim. It seems that in present-day Rwanda, though, they have managed to resolve its conflicts for the moment and are currently ranked one of the fastest developing African countries.

Chapter Eleven

Examples of Countries in Africa After Independence

North Africa

Many people seem to forget that Égypt is a part of Africa. Once one of the most powerful civilizations in the world, Egypt is currently a major tourist attraction and an Islamic nation due to its proximity to the Arab regions of the world. Although Egypt was colonized by the British, the Muslim Brotherhood made an alliance to turn away the people from "evil Western influence." Egypt is heavily involved in Middle East politics. In 1948 it joined Iraq, Jordan, and Syria in attacking Israel. The lackluster performance of the army would be the beginning of the end of the monarchy in Egypt. In 1954 British troops left Egypt ending British rule, although technically, British rule ended in 1922. During British rule, the people of Egypt were forced to dress like the British, which they stopped after the end of the rule. In modern times technically, you can wear whatever you want, but women are generally expected to be modest and wear headscarves, and people are required to remove their shoes before entering religious buildings. Even though I'm paper women have equal rights to men, they are still generally paid less for the same amount of work or more.

Morocco gained its independence from France in 1955. Or would be in 1956 when France fully relinquished its power over Morocco. Morocco was ruled by a royal family, and the head in power after independence was King Hassan II. The king's rule was marked by political unrest and the violent thwarting of all opposition to his rule. After the death of King Hassan II, his son believed more in reform, and progress took over. King Mohammed VI caused significant progress in the country, and its human rights record improved significantly. Despite the reign of King Mohammed VI being better, the Moroccan people still desired a democratically elected leadership. Despite

Morocco being a major tourist attraction, it is still in danger of many terrorist attacks and bombings.

West Africa

Ghana was the first country to gain independence, and its leader Kwame Nkrumah saw it as the spearhead for freedom for the rest of Africa. Nkrumah tried to set up a form of African socialism which eventually led to him being overthrown by his detractors who did not share his ideologies. This would see the country go through a series of coups as people desperately tried to attain power. In 1992, Ghana would have its first democratically elected leader since its various coups, Jerry Rawlings. Under Rawlings, the country saw much political and economic progress despite that many viewed his leadership as authoritarian. For a while, Ghana would have peaceful democratic elections until John Mahama. There were several allegations of electoral fraud during Mahama's time, coupled with an economy caused by a decrease in the cost of Ghana's natural resources, such as the cocoa that it exported. Under Ghana's current president, Nana Addo Dankwa Akufo-Addo, the nation has been building itself up economically, starting with banning the exportation of cocoa to companies like Cadbury, which has been paying sick money for those resources, and

Ghana will start to produce its own chocolate to compete on the international market.

Senegal is known as "the gateway to Africa." It was once a part of Ghana and then the Mail federation. Senegal gained independence by breaking away from the Mali Federation and joining with French Soudan. It was ruled by a joint presidency until one president tried to overthrow the other. The attempt failed. Senegal would then go under the rule of Abdou Diouf. Diouf would lose power in a peaceful transition and democratic elections to Abdoulaye Wade. Because Sénégal has largely managed to remain peaceful since its independence, it is often a participant in international peacekeeping and an example of tranquil elections.

East Africa

Kenya is one of the more diverse and beautiful countries in Africa and often the face of East Africa. The safaris that Africa is so well-known for are most likely based in Kenya. Because of European missionary efforts, much of the population is Catholic but also has a significant population of Muslims. The national language of Kenya and many of the countries in East, Southern, and Central Africa are Swahili which is why Swahili is promoted as a language that should be spoken throughout the continent of Africa. After independence, Jomo Kenyatta became president of Kenya, and only one party was recognized in Kenya for thirty years. There was contention over land ownership, where many of the indigenous Kenyan people killed and raided the farms of white peoples in the country, leading to a mass exodus to the south of Africa. Many of the people that moved away from Kenya were of British origin or part of the Afrikaans tribe (which originated from the Netherlands).

Somalia being so close in proximity to the Middle East is an Islamic Nation despite the efforts of Christian missionaries. Somalia is notable for having faced astronomical difficulties since its independence. It is one of Africa's poorest countries, having been fraught with civil war, drought, and border disputes for decades. Unfortunately, it also has one of the world's lowest literacy rates and highest infant death rates. Border disputes would be the reason that it would sever diplomatic ties with Great Britain in 1963. It would go on to try and become allies with the Soviet Union and become part of the

Arab League, but its internal conflicts have cost the country peace and progress.

Tanzania, after independence, has developed into a peaceful nation that attracts many tourists with its beautiful natural environment and beaches. The people are known to be friendly, with the majority speaking Swahili. Much of Africa's coastal trade happens at its seaport of Dar es Salaam.

Central Africa

The Democratic Republic of Congo is one of Africa's most mineral and natural resource-rich countries. Fruits naturally grow to astronomical sizes, mines are rich with diamonds, gold, silver, and many other precious stones, and the climate is favorable. Unfortunately, it has had some of the worst internal conflicts regardless of having one of the largest United Nations presences in Africa. DRC's rich natural wealth has attracted war from neighboring African countries, and they have also seen an influx of refugees from Rwanda. Its instability has been made worse by a corrupt government where at some point power of the nation was passed on from father to son without elections taking place. The war and turmoil in the nation have made people of Congolese origin internationally recognized as refugees. At some point, families would make sure their girl children were sent out to live abroad due to the exponentially high levels of rape in the nation. In the past decade, there has been an increase in Congolese returning to their home country to try and rebuild it since the inauguration of its current president Felix Tshisekedi.

After independence, Angola went through a season of civil war but was aided by an army from Zaire, The United States, and South Africa in 1974. Cuba favored the party that they opposed, leading to Angola being separated into two regions for a period of time. These separate states didn't last long as Cuba's backed side took over the war. The ensuing war would last for decades, killing millions. Present-day Angola has a huge wealth gap between the haves and have-nots, with a large part of its population in the diaspora. The majority of Angolans speak Portuguese and often immigrate to Portugal. At the moment, an entire generation does not speak any indigenous Angolan language and only Portuguese, which possibly means that some of the indigenous languages of Angola have gone extinct or are endangered.

Southern Africa

South Africa would be the last country in Africa to attain independence. They would go through a unique form of colonialism called apartheid which is still rated as one of the most inhumane systems of governance that have ever existed. Despite being the most economically stable country in Africa, the effects of apartheid still linger, and there's a disparity between white and black people's quality of life. This has caused tensions that sometimes escalate to the wanton murder of white/Afrikaans farmers and the demonization of the "haves." This has led to numerous problems, such as high crime rates, home invasions/farm invasions, and xenophobia. Despite that, South Africa hosted the 2010 World Cup and continues to strive to remain the best economy in Africa and try to improve its safety. One party has been consistently voted into power since it gained independence in 1994 (ANC). Despite its drawbacks, South Africa is known to be a beautiful country that hosts much of Africa's diaspora communities, especially Nigeria and Zimbabwe. It is home to one of the world's best-ranked universities, the University of Cape Town.

Zimbabwe is South Africa's neighbor and has been through a tumultuous time as a nation. Zimbabwe was formerly the "breadbasket of Africa," but due to bad governance and misrule by the ruling political party and sanctions (whose existence is disputed), the economy has collapsed on numerous occasions. Presently the population of Zimbabweans outside their countries is rivaling the population in the country. With a defunct banking system and few job opportunities, many Zimbabweans seek opportunities abroad. Despite that, Zimbabweans are known to be highly educated (one of the good things Mugabe did at the beginning of his reign was to offer free education up to tertiary level for Zimbabweans) and hard workers. The country is known to be very peaceful despite there having been numerous opportunities for civil war. In 2017, Mugabe was ousted from power, and the people hoped for a brighter future with his successor Emerson Mnangagwa. So far, it seems Mnangagwa is cut from the same dictatorial clothe as Mugabe, and there are hopes to oust the entire political party, ZANU-PF, that bred both Mugabe and Mnangagwa.

Chapter Twelve

Where Africa is Now

Africa has been through a tumultuous time, and all of its countries are newly independent. Despite a lot of the turmoil that has come with the after-effects of colonialism, many people predict that many countries in Africa will become world powers once it overcomes the biggest issues to their progress, such as bad governance and corruption. The people of the continent are known to be educated and desire a better society. Zimbabwe, which was once known as Africa's breadbasket, is uncertain since its long-reigning president Robert Mugabe was forcibly removed from power.Rwanda has a growing economy that is attracting a lot of foreign investment, although its capital city is developing at a much faster rate than any other part of the country leading to disproportionate standards of living.

In 2010 South Africa hosted the FIFA World Cup, which garnered increased interest in all the southern African countries. During that time, the value of the rand went up and would trade for approximately 1 United States dollar for nine rands. That was a boost to South Africa's tourism economy because, for a long time, it had been viewed as a country that was too dangerous to travel to. The economy experienced a decline in the subsequent years and wasn't able to keep tourism at the same level as in 2010, but its major tourist city, Cape Town, was able to branch out and is currently considered the Silicon Valley of Africa and has in the past two years surpassed Johannesburg as the financial center of Africa. The Democratic Republic of Congo is still war-torn and full of conflict in many regions but has seen many refugees and asylum seekers return to their country to try and build it up after building savings in other countries. Nigeria is also considered a major financial hub of Africa despite internal wars and conflicts. Nigeria has the largest African diaspora community due to economic, political, and religious instability. This is countered by Nigeria, which also has the largest number of billionaires, millionaires, and highly educated people in Africa. Africa has had high levels of diasporans, but the past decades have seen a large number continentally returning to their countries for numerous reasons. Some of the most common reasons are getting away from racism, self-actualization, affordable housing, etc. The issue of racism against black people has become such a huge issue for many people in the community that many non-African black people are also immigrating and relocating to African countries. Nigeria and Ghana have created programs that make it easier for non-African blacks, particularly black Americans, to relocate to Africa.

In July of 2022, Kenya opened the Nairobi International Financial Centre, which seeks to make it the preferred destination of the international business community, mirroring the Dubai model of success. The center aims to earn about $2 billion in incremental, cumulative investments by 2030.

On the downside, African countries are still under a form of quasi-colonialism, such as Cameroon. Although it officially gained independence on the 1st of January 1960, France still has control of most of its economy and major industries, making it difficult for local Cameroonians to get employment or earn a living above a certain level.

Africa is a diverse and wondrous continent with a deep and complicated history. At the moment, there is hope that despite all of its problems, the determination and work ethic of the African people will overcome all obstacles and help the continent compete on an international level.

Chapter Thirteen

Conclusion

It has become a habit of many societies and people around the world to refer to Africa as just one entity with one identity. Many people, even some Africans, believe that if you know one African country, you know them all. Unfortunately, the history of Africa is often not taught in schools, and what people know of modern Africa is often poverty-stricken children with kwashiorkor waiting desperately for well-wishers and good Samaritans from more developed countries to come and save them. The problem with that image being portrayed is that, at the end of the day, societies around the world end up believing that there is nothing good coming out of Africa.

While it is true that there are very sad levels of poverty and lack of food security in some parts of the continent, each part of it has a rich history and dynamic that shows that it has a multidimensional identity. Just like America was once promoted as the greatest country in the world with the best standard of living and was made to look better than it was, while communities like those that live in the Appalachian region that are poverty-stricken and live on food stamps were often completely left out of the American narrative. Similarly, the positive aspects of Africa have been largely left out of the African narrative to the excessive advertisement of its vices.

Africa's many different civilizations were, in their time, world powers. Almost every African country had a thriving pre-colonial society, had to fight to gain freedom, and also showed promise in rebuilding post-colonialism despite spats of war and corruption. Modern African countries are developing their own identities and ways of running life amidst international uncertainty. Some African countries are becoming hubs for international immigration and business deals, such as Kenya's goal to become a central business hub like Dubai.

Besides poverty, there are also Africans who are using their own resources to give housing, food, and education to hundreds of youth in their country who are orphaned and destitute. Many people use limited resources to make their own cars, solar panels, and other inventions that conventionally use many more resources. Africa's story is still a work in progress, but the people and communities are optimistic that one day it might be a world power.

Chapter Fourteen

"Discuss with Friends and Family"

Discussion Question

How do you think African communities are developing amidst many problems? Does that mean that a nation's development rests on the people? Or, as in the case of Morocco, does the government play a larger role in a nation's progress?

Discussion Question

South Africa was the last country to gain independence. It probably went through the worst type of colonial rule through apartheid. Do you think apartheid was so bad because the colonizers learned from previous colonies that had gained independence?

Discussion Question

In her bestselling novel. Alexandra Fuller confesses that her white parents moved from Kenya to South Rhodesia in an attempt to retain one white-run country in Africa. What do you think was the logic behind this? Do you think that settlers were unaware of the impact of colonialism on the locals?

Discussion Question

"Modern Africa seems to be caught between a painful past it can't let go of, a tumultuous present, and an uncertain future," How far do you agree with that statement? Should the past be let go of?

Discussion Question

Kwame Nkrumah wanted to lead Ghana into socialism. Do you think that system would be sustainable? Do you think he thought socialism was best because colonialism was basically a product of capitalism?

Discussion Question

Football star Sadie Mane has used the fortune he gained from playing football to build schools and hospitals and develop his home country. Do you think that he's been able to do that because Senegal is generally a peace-loving country? Do you think he's hit blockades because of corruption?

Discussion Question

Zimbabwe is said to have one of the highest literacy rates in Africa but also one of the highest levels of poverty. Does education truly equal emancipation in this case? Explain.

Discussion Question

Where do you think South Africa and Zimbabwe are headed in the future after all the political turmoil they've been through? Do you think that the two countries are connected? Is Zimbabwe reliant on South Africa?

Chapter Fifteen

"Test Your Knowledge"

Quiz Question

1. **True or False:** South Africa was the last country in Africa to gain independence and is also the most economically developed country in Africa. Its two major cities are the financial hubs of Africa.

2. **True or False:** Part of Nigeria's charm is its rich food culture. Many people are enamored with jollof rice and egusi soup. Food tourism is a major way that countries are building relationships in the modern day.

3. **True or False:** Kwame Nkrumah wanted a capitalistic form of government. He believed that for the people to have true freedom, the state should not interfere that much.

4. **True or False:** Winston Churchill was ecstatic to give Africa its independence. He believed that keeping Africa as a

colony was inhumane. False. Churchill was against the end of British rule.

5. **True or False:** Kenya has the best safaris in Africa. All of the best wildlife is found there.

6. **True or False:** Afrikaans people originated from the Netherlands and settled in many places but moved further south as more African countries gained independence. The largest modern population is in South Africa.

7. **True or False**: Ghana became a benchmark for African independence. Great Britain fought hard to try and repress the Ghanaian revolution but eventually gave them self-governance.

8. **True or False:** Somalia is still trying to gain its footing. There are high levels of poverty and high child mortality that stop the development of the country..

Quiz Answer

1. True

2. True

3. False. Kwame Nkrumah wanted a socialist form of government for Ghana.

4. False. Churchill was against the end of British rule.

5. False: Wildlife is found all over Africa, though the best safaris are in Kenya.

6. True

7. True

8. True

Bibliography (Works Cited)

Part four.A valley in South Africa+
<https://unsplash.com/photos/04-C1NZk1hE>

Part 3, The Wild Fields Of Kenya,
<https://unsplash.com/photos/T-LfvX-7IVg>

Part 2. Pictured above are locals walking up Kilimanjaro.
<https://images.unsplash.com/photo-1521150932951-303a95503ed3?>

Part 2. Pictured above are the members of the Kavango tribe of Namibia. <https://images.unsplash.com/photo-1615277716473-64285a2356df?>

Part 3. Pictured above is scenery from Morocco.
<https://images.unsplash.com/photo-1527338611623-4e242563220a?>

Part 3. Pictured above is a Zimbabwean Girl Protesting War in Africa. <https://images.unsplash.com/photo-1646765036313-05d81f49d7f3?ixlib=rb-4.0.3&dl=ben-masora-1KqGR_bhluE-unsplash.jpg&w=640&q=80&fm=jpg&crop=entropy&cs=tinysrgb>

Part 4. Pictured above is Cape Town, currently the financial hub of Africa. <https://images.unsplash.com/photo-1580060839134-75a5edca2e99?>

Bonus Download

Want to Fill Your Digital Library for Free?

Every purchase comes with FREE bonus downloads!
Download yours now by clicking the 'Get it Now' button.

Get it Now

Scan Your Phone to open QR code

Final Words From the Author...

Dear Reader,

It was my utmost privilege performing a deep dive to bringing this book for you today.

Before saying goodbye, I'd like to take opportunity to offer you one final gift. If you've enjoyed this book, may I ask for a small review?

If you do, I'll send you for FREE a most cherished and valuable gift as a way of showing my utmost appreciation:

Bestsellers Top 7 Treasure Box

These are my personal bestsellers sold at bookstores valued at ~$30USD, my gift to you absolutely FREE.

To claim your gift:

1. Leave a review where the book was purchased
2. Send a screenshot to irvinepress@mail.com
3. Receive your gift of **Bestsellers Top 7 Treasure Box**

Sincerely,

History Encounters

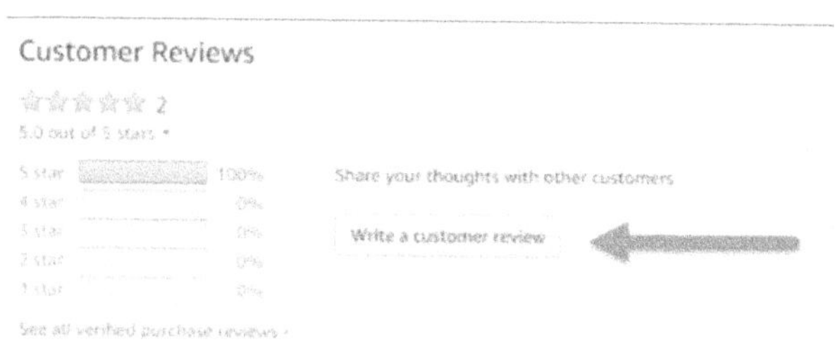

THANK YOU